Edmund Arrowsmith

by
John S. Hogan

In Memory of
Very Rev. Canon Francis J. Ripley

All booklets are published thanks to the
generous support of the members of the
Catholic Truth Society

CATHOLIC TRUTH SOCIETY
PUBLISHERS TO THE HOLY SEE

Contents

Introduction 3

Early Years 10

Douai 20

Mission 30

Jesuit 37

Betrayal 42

Trial 48

Witness 58

Glory 71

All rights reserved. First published 2016 by The Incorporated Catholic Truth Society, 40-46 Harleyford Road London SE11 5AY Tel: 020 7640 0042 Fax: 020 7640 0046. © The Incorporated Catholic Truth Society. Images: Page 38: Portrait of Edmund Arrowsmith, copy from an original portrait from St Mary's Church, Wigan. Courtesy of the Archives of the Society of Jesus (British Province), Mount Street, London. Page 60: Engraving of Edmund Arrowsmith's execution, from Matthias Tanner SJ's 'Societas Iesu usque ad sanguinis', 1675. Courtesy of Archives of the Society of Jesus (British Province), Mount Street, London.

ISBN 978 1 78469 121 9

Introduction

The children stand shivering in the cold. It was well into the night when they were awoken by the banging on the door. Thrown out of bed, now they huddle together disorientated, tied two by two; they watch as their home is ransacked. The priest-hunters tear through the house; swords are applied to every nook and corner, cupboards cleared, walls pounded to see if priest holes have been constructed in the fabric of the building. As usual, they find nothing. No doubt later, as they are cleaning up, certain items will be missing; perhaps they appealed to the searchers and were secreted away or just 'confiscated'. Leaving as suddenly as they came, they take mother and father with them: the children are left standing outside dressed only in their nightclothes. It was not the first time, nor, probably, the last. The eldest, Brian, takes charge of his siblings and leads them to a neighbour's house where he knows they will find refuge, warmth, and a little comfort after the ordeal. Their parents will be back in the morning after they have paid the fine to regain their liberty, and the priest-hunters' wages - they have to be compensated for their night's work and it is the victims who have to pay them. Life will resume its normal course, until another knock is heard in the middle of the night.

Such was the childhood experience of the Arrowsmith
children, and indeed many Catholic children in the years
following the establishment of a new church in England.
The post-Reformation years were difficult for adherents of
the 'Old Faith'. Refusing to embrace the King's religion
and the Queen's 'settlement' they held on, paying fines for
non-attendance at state church services, gathering in secret
for Mass, hiding priests, adapting to ever greater poverty.

Recusants and Catholicism in Lancashire

In the north of England there were more recusants than
down south. Though monarchs and their servants did
everything they could to make them conform, Northerners
remained faithful: they were strong willed and clever. By
the time young Brian Arrowsmith and his siblings joined
the ranks of the persecuted, the Catholics of the north knew
better than to trust a monarch. In the years following the
religious revolution they had launched what could have
been a successful coup against a reigning monarch. The
Pilgrimage of Grace in 1536 and 1537 had been an appeal
to Henry VIII to allow them to remain Catholic. The king
resorted to treachery to foil them; they were loyal, they
believed a king's promises and they paid the price with
their lives.

They were still loyal, as they tried to assure Henry's
insecure daughter, Elizabeth; but their first allegiance was
to the One who had sovereignty over their souls. Though

a worldly queen should try to claim it, her realm did not extend to their souls or their consciences. Too many had died; there had been too much bloodshed. What was said to be a reformation seemed more like a revolution, one in stages, backwards and forwards, with death being the only constant. Many of those facilitating it were not so much men and women of principle, but of ambition. Henry dismantled the Church and her monasteries to enrich himself; his son Edward, though sickly and dependent, changed the face of English Christianity. Mary, his Catholic daughter, tried to turn the clock back, but time and that fierce Tudor streak hobbled her efforts which disintegrated when her sister, Elizabeth, succeeded her.

Elizabeth's settlement

Elizabeth imposed a settlement, a half-way house, she claimed, between her sister's orthodox Catholicism and her brother's Protestantism. In reality she had more of her father in her and the new established church was centred on her rather than being an accommodation between Catholics and Calvinists. She sought to enforce this settlement by means of law, and throughout her reign various acts were passed to gradually squeeze out Catholicism. She interpreted adherence to the 'Old Faith', as Catholicism was called, as an action depriving her of allegiance that was her due as sovereign. Those priests and laity condemned for their fidelity to Catholicism were arraigned for their presumed attack on the queen's sovereignty in her own realm. At the beginning of her reign she said: "I have no desire to make windows into men's souls" meaning she had no interest in looking into anyone's conscience, she only asked that her subjects respect her and be loyal. In reality, however, she did seek to look into the souls, hearts and minds of her subjects and demanded that their first allegiance, including their spiritual fealty, be to her.

In her first year she repealed all of Mary's legislative acts, re-enacting those of her father and brother, coupled with a new Act of Supremacy with oath attached. Another act outlawed the Roman Missal and established Archbishop Cranmer's Book of Common Prayer as the only liturgical text to be used in church. For the next forty years more acts were passed to ensure Elizabeth's subjects attended Anglican services. Priests were banned from the realm: it was not only high treason for a priest to be in England, it was treasonous for an Englishman, a subject of the queen, to be ordained. Other acts made it treasonous for a Jesuit to be in England, to bring Papal Bulls into the country, to print books that were critical of the queen, and, in an act of 1581, to convert to Catholicism. Those who fell foul of the new laws were fined, hanged, or subject to the most cruel method of execution of all: hanging, drawing and quartering. These laws remained throughout the reigns of her successors the Stuart kings James I and Charles I. Under Charles they were for the most part ignored.

A noble, if weak, king, Charles abhorred the idea of killing his subjects on account of their religion. As his power waned, so too the toleration he hoped to instil.

The story of Edmund

This was the world in which St Edmund Arrowsmith lived, the little Brian of the story. To understand him and his ministry we must understand the times and their effect on him. As he stood as a little boy huddled with his shivering siblings, drawing them in to himself, the priest was born. In his short life and ministry he sought to give shelter to a suffering people, to surround them in his priestly embrace. He risked his life to console, to comfort, to teach and bring to Christ a people who endured great hardship and were prepared to endure much worse for the sake of their faith. Edmund did not surrender to hatred. He was a man of principle, often of few words; those words he did utter were wise, strong and true, emerging from a heart that was not only convinced of the truth of the Catholic faith, but one which was united with the founder of that faith, Jesus Christ. As Christ was his refuge in trial and sorrows, he sought to bring his people to that same refuge so they too would find the strength they needed to remain true.

One of Edmund's first biographers, his Jesuit confère, Fr Cornelius Murphy, SJ, writes, "We have little left concerning Father Arrowsmith, after what inquiry could be made, besides what relates to his happy suffering for the Faith": much of the martyr's life is shrouded in mystery; he was a man who lived in the shadows by necessity. There are some original sources which are the basis of this brief biography, the most important being a contemporary account published in 1630, two years after his martyrdom, its writer unknown. This account was redacted and supplemented by Murphy and published in 1737. Other sources include Bishop Richard Challoner's *Memoirs of Missionary Priests* (1874); Br Henry Foley's *Records of the English Province of the Society of Jesus* (1875) and Dom Bede Camm's *Forgotten Shrines* (1910). Among general histories of the era, Fr John Gerard's *Autobiography of an Elizabethan* offers a first-hand account of the life of a missionary priest in penal England, a valuable resource which allows us a glimpse of what Edmund's life must have been like.

Heroic priesthood

Edmund worked in the shadows, in silence, hidden away with his people, serving them and loving them with a fatherly heart. He was English to the core, a proud son of the north; he loved his country and prayed for it just before he died, forgiving those who had brought him to the scaffold. Like St Thomas More, however, his love for his country and its queen could not supersede his love for Christ and the loyalty he knew was required of a son of the Church. He lived in the midst of the truth and he could not deny it; he could see that a true settlement could only be found in embracing the truth and living the life of Christian discipleship - in rendering to Christ our total allegiance. In the eyes of many this made him a traitor, a difficult subject; in the view of others he was a patriot, a man of principle, a martyr. This latter view has been confirmed by God with his glorification, and in the times we live in Edmund's life and example is more relevant than ever. God's raising of his servant to the altars places before the whole Church a model of faithful discipleship in the midst of trial, of heroic priesthood and joyful living of the consecrated life in an age that did not understand it.

Early Years

Thurston Arrowsmith and Nicholas Gerard were men not
only united in their adherence to the Catholic faith but also
through the marriage of their children Robert and Margery
in 1584. One a yeoman farmer, the other a member of the
distinguished Gerard family, these committed Catholics
conferred on their children, and eventually their grandson,
a legacy of simple, humble faith tied to a dogged resistance
to any attempt to have them shake it off.

Thurston often landed himself in hot water with the
authorities for his persistent and stubborn fidelity to
'Popery'. He had been in and out of prison for refusing to
attend Protestant services. He had been fined, roughly treated
and robbed by priest-hunters, his home ransacked at various
intervals in the search for priests or evidence of them. His
last incarceration occurred in 1582, when he was confined
to prison near Salford for the usual offences. This prison,
according to one author, was similar to a concentration camp,
and was established to house "stubborn and contemptuous
recusants".[1] In this imprisonment Thurston endured various
deprivations: in the words of Bishop Challoner: "after loss
of goods, and frequent vexations from the pursuivants, [he]
suffered a long imprisonment, and died in bonds a confessor
of Christ".

Meanwhile, the more genteel Nicholas Gerard was defending the faith in his own way. Both Challoner and Foley describe in their biographies of St Edmund how Nicholas was forcibly brought to church under orders from his brother, Sir Thomas Gerard.[2] The 'adventure' Sir Thomas organised for his brother was staged when Nicholas was debilitated by a severe attack of gout and more easily managed, or so it was thought. Nicholas was carried forcibly on a palette to the local Anglican Sunday service where, situated in the aisle, the old man refused to join the worshippers in their prayers but equally refused to remain quiet, offering worship of his own by singing the psalms in Latin at the top of his voice. He was quickly expelled from the church and taken home to the relief of the congregation and the vicar whose hard-wrought sermon had disappeared during its delivery somewhere between the pulpit and the pews, victim to the inflections of the Catholic psalter as determinedly intoned by the pious Nicholas. Little else is known of Nicholas's life and death, but his example and fidelity found admiration and imitation in the lives of his daughter and his grandson Edmund.

Brian and his family

That grandson, Robert and Margery's first child, was born in 1585, on the 11th June according some sources. He was baptised according to Catholic rites and called Brian.[3] At the time of the birth his parents were living in Haydock,

Robert having inherited his father's farm. Yeoman farmers owned their own land; they were commoners rather than members of the gentry or aristocracy. A yeoman would have owned at least a hundred acres and some were quite wealthy. Their prestige and position in society allowed them to serve on juries and vote in elections for the Knights of the Shire; they could also hold various offices including constables of the parish, churchwardens and overseers of the parish. Some had been elected chief constables of districts, bailiffs and even High Sheriffs. Robert and Margery would have had standing in the community and would not have been poor, or at least they should not have been; fines and other measures taken against Catholics diminished what would have been a comfortable life.

Brian's birth was followed in the years to come by the births of three others, of which one is known to have also been a boy: this son is known to have become a Benedictine monk. Growing up in one of the most Catholic areas of England at that time, Brian's boyhood years were marked by the feasts and seasons of the Church's year coupled harmoniously with the agricultural year. Nearby a priest, ordained during the reign of Mary I, lived and ministered in secret. This priest offered Mass, administered the sacraments and offered spiritual care to local Catholics, so Brian and his family would have attended Mass at least each Sunday. The priest also catechised the children, taught them Latin and encouraged them in their spiritual lives.

From his early years Brian demonstrated a natural piety which was nourished by a fervent family life and Catholic traditions that had been handed down for generations. George Beck, late Archbishop of Liverpool, once wrote of him that he was "a fine example of the traditional faith of the Lancashire people": he was a child of Catholic England and her rich spirituality. It was perhaps no surprise then that, despite the dangers of the age in which he lived, this child would discern and nurture a call to the priesthood.

A rural childhood

Though little is known of his early life beyond a few facts, the regular patterns of a typical Elizabethan rural childhood would have found resonance in his boyhood. His parents, siblings and extended family would have played an important role in his life. The solid independence of the yeomanry would have been instilled in him, giving him a sense not only of his own worth, but of the inherent value of others. This sense of liberty would have been balanced by the way of life lived by his mother's family, the Gerards. Given the strict social hierarchy of the time, his parents' marriage was exceptional; many would have considered Margery as having married beneath her, Robert being of a lower social class. That never troubled her, and it would not have troubled Brian, indeed it may have led him to develop a healthy scepticism of the class system; extended family life would have seen him drift seamlessly through classes. That said, the Gerard ancestral traits were in him: he was an heir to an honourable tradition, descended from worthy men and women. That must surely have given him a sense of confidence and, coupled with the independent yeomanry spirit, might well explain the extraordinary nature of the man he would become: one with an assertive, self-assured and strong personality. The legacy of fidelity to the Catholic faith and the witness given by relatives from both sides of his family would have had an effect on him. Thurston and Nicholas's doughty defence of their faith; the martyrdom of his distant cousin, Fr Miles Gerard of the Ince branch of the family; the stories of his cousin, Fr John Gerard, offered valiant models which would have helped form the mind and heart of a young boy for whom heroism was not a distant ideal, but a way of life.

Work and leisure time

Work started early for Brian and his siblings, as it usually does for those reared on a farm, chores giving way, as he grew older, to more demanding work. Farms were for the most part self-sufficient, and the local community was small and tight-knit, so locals depended on each other, particularly at harvest time. With the high population of Catholics in Lancashire, community bonds would have been deeper given the hostility they had to face. There was the regular market day when Brian would have accompanied his parents to sell surplus produce and buy what they needed. As money could be in short supply, bartering was the basis of many transactions, and there would also have been a reliance on local skilled labour; through such social transitions Brian's circle of acquaintances would have grown as he got older and was more involved in community life.

But it was not all work. Elizabethans loved their leisure time, and when night fell they had a little time to relax before going to bed. Typical farming households would have spent evenings in conversation or, in good Catholic homes, in prayer. Stories, songs and games would have entertained them, and given Brian's noted wit and sense of humour, jokes and fun must have had an honoured place in the Arrowsmith home. Feasts always had an important place in Catholic England, and the recusants of Lancashire would have aimed to keep traditions alive, not only to mark sacred times and preserve their identity, but to console and renew themselves through the mysteries they commemorated. Penitential times were faithfully observed and then brought to an end with family gatherings for banquets: increased poverty, thanks to fines, would have reduced the profligacy of feasts, but certainly not the sentiments.

Studies

Brian attended the local school at Seneley Green, later Ashton Grammar School, founded by Sir Thomas Gerard in 1587. As a school it conformed to the state religion with Anglican teachers teaching the children not only their reading and writing, but also loyalty to the Crown and the state religion. Given his open and friendly personality, Brian impressed his school masters. He applied himself diligently to his work; he had a natural intelligence and keen curiosity. It is noted by some biographers that his intelligence was somewhat dulled there; though he did well in his studies he seems to have become bored with what was being taught; it was when he went to university in Douai that his intellectual abilities were reawakened and he thrived academically.

Brian and his siblings walked to school each day, about a mile each way, but this time was not wasted. The natural piety of the young Arrowsmiths led them to pray on the way to and from school. Early biographies relate how Brian prayed the Little Hours of Our Lady on the way to school and Vespers and Compline on the way home in the evening. Given that traditions and learning were often passed on within an oral culture, it is no surprise that Brian and his siblings would have known these prayers off by heart - they were probably the spiritual staple of the family. Challoner tells us in the *Memoirs* that as soon as Brian came home from school he would "withdraw into his oratory [in the farmhouse] and there perform his customary devotions of the Jesus Psalter, the seven psalms etc". This reveals not just a particularly devout boy, but a spiritually precocious one whose heart seemed set on a life of devotion rather than a life on the farm.

As well-known Catholics in the area, the Arrowsmiths were subject to constant harassment from local magistrates and priest-hunters, or pursuivants as they were also known. These tormentors knew they were operating in a region that was still overwhelmingly Catholic and realised that for their own safety they had to be careful not to transgress a line; house searches and fines, however, were well within that line. For refusing to attend Sunday Service at the local Anglican church the Arrowsmiths had to pay numerous fines. Night raids were common.

Difficulties for the family

Impoverished through fines and imprisonment, Robert realised that the family could not survive on what was left of the farming income: he would have to emigrate. There were plenty of opportunities for those willing to fight as mercenaries in the various wars devastating Europe. With his younger brother Peter, Robert left England for the Low Countries leaving Margery to manage the farm. When they arrived, to their dismay, they were pressed into service against Catholic Spain. Foley records that the two brothers, when in battle, deliberately fired into the air so as not to shoot a Catholic soldier. They later managed to enlist in the Spanish army thanks to the efforts of an Englishman, Sir William Stanley, who was in service to the King of Spain. On one campaign Peter was wounded in battle and moved to Brussels to recuperate; however, he succumbed to his

wounds and was buried there. Robert sought out his elder
brother Edmund who was working at the English College,
Douai, then temporarily sited in Reims. In their meeting the
two brothers may well have discussed, among other things,
Brian's plans; no doubt the pious uncle encouraged the
child's father to foster this divine call. After their reunion
Robert returned to Haydock; they would never meet again.
Robert died soon after he returned to his family, just before
the turn of the century.

After Robert's death, Margery found herself in difficult
circumstances, both personal and financial. Burdened
by penalties the farm did not produce enough to provide
an adequate living for her family, and she had little
opportunity to supplement her income. Charity, though,
was not far away: the local priest came to her rescue and
took Brian into his service. His work as a servant would
be complemented with further study to prepare him for
seminary, but it also allowed him to see first-hand how a
missionary priest lived and ministered.

The times were changing: Queen Elizabeth died on the
24th March 1603; the era of 'Gloriana' the Virgin Queen
was finally passing. Before her death was announced a
messenger was dispatched to Scotland to inform King
James VI, son of Mary Queen of Scots, that as Elizabeth's
closest relative he was now King of England. Hopes among
English Catholics rose - this son of the martyred Catholic
Queen of Scots, now King James I of England and Ireland,

would surely deal kindly with his mother's co-religionists. Would the penal laws be set aside and Catholics permitted to practise their faith in freedom?

Douai

The accession of James Stuart as King of England was welcomed by most in the realm. It was not just Catholics who uttered a sigh of relief at Elizabeth's death; she was not universally mourned - the enchanting myth of the great Elizabeth would only emerge with the passing of time, and perhaps thanks to the failures of the Stuarts. The new monarchy brought new hopes of peace and tolerance; but whatever hopes the Catholics of England had, as James settled on his English throne and maintained the status quo, they quickly faded to be replaced, among some, by anger. This anger would blow up, metaphorically only, with the Gunpowder Plot in November 1605 designed to assassinate James and wipe out parliament. Instead of tolerance, Catholics found themselves demonised once again. Tyburn would prove to be as busy under James as it was under Elizabeth.

As Guy Fawkes and his allies were conspiring, Brian was hatching a secret plan himself. As he turned twenty, he decided the time had come to pursue his vocation. As his mother had no objection, with the help of the priest he served, he tried to arrange admission to a seminary in Spain. Various difficulties presented themselves and his hopes of entering a seminary there were gradually eaten away. But there was another option - his uncle's seminary, the English College at Douai. Brian may well have seen the work of providence in all of this: not only was Douai the place where his uncle had laboured, it was also the alma mater of Fr Edmund Campion one of Brian's, and Catholic England's, heroes. Douai was well known for its singular priests. By 1605, beginning with Fr Cuthbert Mayne, 126 of its alumni had been martyred, including Campion, Robert Southwell (the famous Jesuit poet) and Brian's own distant cousin Miles Gerard.

But there remained the problem of how to get out of England. Normally one had to obtain a licence to leave the country, and that meant explaining why one needed to leave. A young man of twenty from a known recusant family in the north would have raised suspicions that he was travelling to enter a seminary. The furore over the Gunpowder Plot did not help either. Spies haunted the ports and they were known to take passage on ships, mingling with the passengers to identify priests or potential priests. We have no details of how Brian did actually get to Douai - like much of his life his journey takes place in secret so as not to attract attention. He is known to have arrived by the winter of 1605.

Seminary for the English mission

Douai, in present-day France, but then part of Spanish Flanders, was the seat of a new university founded in 1559 by King Philip II of Spain. The University of Douai was modelled on Louvain, comprising five faculties: theology, canon law, civil law, medicine and arts or humanities. The choice of first Chancellor, an Englishman, Dr Richard Smith, was a decision which would prove symbolic of the university's relationship with England and the suffering Church there. It soon became a magnet for English Catholics. Some former students of Oxford and Cambridge even staffed the faculties. When Lancashire priest William Allen was attempting to found a seminary to train priests for the English mission, Douai, with its new university with eminent staff and a large number of exiled English Catholics living in the town, seemed to be the perfect place.

William Allen was one of the most dynamic churchmen of his generation. Born during the reign of Henry VIII in 1532, he benefited from the restoration of Catholicism under Mary I, becoming a Master of Arts at Oxford and receiving the tonsure to become a Canon of York Minster. Following Elizabeth's accession he refused to take the Oath of Supremacy, but was allowed to remain at Oxford until 1561 when he went into self-imposed exile. Finishing his theological studies in Louvain, though not yet a priest, he was forced to return to England due to ill health; he used the opportunity to work on the mission in Lancashire. Convinced that most people had become Protestant not through conviction but through sheer monarchical force, he considered Elizabeth's settlement temporary and that her subjects could be reconciled to the Church through the ministry of zealous, learned priests. Forced to flee Lancashire, he hid out in Norfolk for a short time before leaving for the Continent; he would never return to his native land. He was ordained to the priesthood in Flanders in 1565.

The English College at Douai

The English College was born in Allen's heart as he spent time in Rome in 1567. If England was to be converted back to the faith it needed good priests, and a good seminary was necessary to train them. Encouraged by a professor of law at Douai University, and with financial assistance from friends and communities of Benedictines in Flanders, he bought a house and on 29th September 1568 the English College was inaugurated. Allen would nurture his foundation with fatherly care and fiery zeal. He would later participate in establishing a second college in Rome in 1575, the Venerable English College. For his work he was created cardinal in 1587. Philip II of Spain, in his plans for England following his invasion of 1588, had tipped Allen to become Archbishop of Canterbury, but the failure of the Spanish Armada put an end to that.

Fr Cornelius Murphy, writing about the English College, noted that it was "a Seminary of many illustrious Martyrs, and zealous labourers in the Vineyard, learned and pious persons who have adorned the Church with their lives and their learned works, stocked Religious Orders with able subjects, and particularly enriched the least Society of Jesus with many eminent personages from that seat of piety and learning". Among those eminent Jesuits was Edmund Campion, who entered the seminary in 1571. Doubling as a teacher and student, Campion taught his brother seminarians while finishing his own degree in Theology, graduating on 21st January 1573. He received minor orders there before moving to Rome and entering the Society of Jesus the following April.

Founding the College, William Allen had a distinct aim: he wanted his priests to be saints, and they had to be if they were to endure the trials and risks of life on the English mission. Given the climate at home, Allen realised that many of his students would be martyred. St Philip Neri was wont to bless the future martyrs when newly ordained English priests were leaving their college in Rome; Allen sought to bless his students with holiness and skill to help them conduct effective ministries and, if it fell to them, to die heroic deaths.

Practical and theological needs

The College was to produce holy, zealous men trained to meet the practical needs of the English mission; the University, where the seminarians attended lectures, was to train them to be scholars and controversialists. Of all the subjects to be studied Allen placed greatest emphasis on Scripture, not only to ground the theological training of his priests but to equip them to offer solid exegesis in their pastoral work. Aware of the divergent interpretations of Scripture that prevailed in England he needed men well grounded in the Word of God. Allen's devotion to the Scriptures would find its manifestation in the eventual publication of the Douai-Reims Bible, a new translation to rival those being produced in England.

Brian was admitted to the English College in December 1605, sharing Allen's intentions and desires for his own formation and ministry. While he had become "dull witted" in the schoolroom his intellect reawakened in Douai - there was now an evangelical and pastoral purpose to his study. In his life as a priest he was intent on following Edmund Campion's example and he made this intention clear when he received the Sacrament of Confirmation soon after his arrival, taking the name Edmund as his confirmation name and deciding that he would be known by that name for the rest of his life. And so the Diary of the English College records that "Edmund Arrowsmith" was admitted to study for the priesthood for the Diocese of Chester. On admission, Edmund took the oath promising that he would return to work on the English mission: Douai was not a college for merely academic pursuits; it was a training ground for heroic missionary priests intent on reconverting their land to its ancient faith.

Life at seminary

The life of a seminarian in Douai was similar to that of seminarians all over the world in every age. The day began at 5 a.m. with prayer and ended with prayer. The spiritual life of the seminarians was guided by able spiritual directors, among whom were Jesuits, included because of Allen's admiration for their learning, ability and holiness. Edmund attended classes in the University each day, his academic programme was to progress from the humanities to philosophy to theology to eventual ordination. College life was austere, but exciting: optimistic young men full of ideals living, learning and training together. Subjects were taught in a practical way, oriented towards mission, evangelisation and disputation. Seminary life was not all work and study as time was allotted each week for rest and recreation: the Lord's Day was held holy, and Thursdays were also free to allow students some time to themselves.

The path to priesthood

Among his fellow seminarians, one who would go on to play an important part in his life was Edward Barlow, who entered in 1608. From the village of Chorlton-cum-Hardy near Manchester, Edward was a member of a prominent Catholic family. His brother William was already in Douai, a member of the Benedictine monastery there. While Edward had enrolled himself in the English College, he was also discerning a monastic vocation.

He would eventually enter the Benedictines in 1612 and return to minister on the English mission where he worked alongside Edmund in Lancashire. A later event in their lives, as we shall see, would suggest that the two formed a close friendship.

Intellectually and spiritually Edmund thrived in Douai, but though he was zealous, his health was not as robust as his intentions. He fell seriously ill a number of times, and twice received the Last Rites. Though he pulled through on both occasions, his body was weak. To assist his recovery those involved in his formation took the decision to send him home in May 1607 to see if his native air would improve his constitution. Devastated, Edmund took the boat back to England and to Haydock where he spent time in convalescence praying that his health would improve enough to allow him return to Douai. His prayers were answered and he re-entered the seminary on 1st August 1608.

Something interesting happened at this time. After he had finished his studies in philosophy Edmund made a retreat according to the Spiritual Exercises of St Ignatius of Loyola. One of the Jesuit spiritual directors of the English College regularly conducted the Exercises for the students as part of their spiritual formation, and the Exercises resonated with Edmund, so much so that he was seriously considering entering the Society of Jesus. Not only was Edmund thinking of entering the Jesuits himself, he was also encouraging a fellow student to go with him. It seems the possibility of a vocation as a Jesuit accompanied him throughout his years at Douai, though in the end he decided to remain at the English College. The oath taken when he entered the seminary binding him to serve the English mission did not prevent him from entering a religious order as long as he was sent to England, but at that time, to be faithful to the oath and his vision for his mission, he remained on track for the secular priesthood.

Preparations for his mission

While all in general was going well, Edmund's health continued to be a concern. Rather than send him home again, and unduly lengthen his training, it was decided, given his competence and ability, to shorten his studies and send him for ordination early. He received the tonsure and minor orders of porter, lector, exorcist and acolyte in the Church of St Nicholas, Douai, on 14th June 1612; he then began his preparation for ordination to the priesthood, for which a date was set for December in the Cathedral at Arras. Early in December he made his way to Arras. On 6th December he was admitted to the subdiaconate, and on 8th December ordained deacon. The next day, Sunday 9th December 1612, the Bishop of Arras, Hermann Ottemberg, ordained Edmund to the priesthood, most likely in the Cathedral of Notre Dame and Saint Vaast.

Following ordination he returned to the English College to make final preparations for his journey home. He would not leave until June of the following year, so he may have continued his studies, made contacts to arrange his passage and plan what he would do and where he would go when he set foot back in England. He would also have been aware that spies were everywhere and that his journey home might well come to the attention of priest-hunters. His first step onto English soil could well be a fatal one - his cousin Miles Gerard had been arrested as he arrived back in England: as his ship was wrecked on the Kent coast priest-hunters were on hand to identify him. Prudence and caution were required, then; for all Edmund knew, he could already be a marked man.

Mission

As secretly as he had left, Edmund, now twenty-eight, returned to England in 1613. The president of the College, Dr Matthew Kellison, sent him and six others out on 17th June with a blessing, knowing they might well be facing incarceration and a horrendous death in the not too distant future. Edmund entered England without incident and he may have made his way home to Haydock to greet his mother whom he had not seen since 1608.

How did Edmund Arrowsmith turn out, after all his adventures and experiences? What was this young priest like? The contemporary account of 1630 describes him as being "a man of mean presence but of great innocency in his life, of great sincerity in his nature, of great sweetness in his conversation, and of great industry in his function and was ever of a cheerful countenance, a most probable sign of an upright and unspotted conscience". A man of "homely carriage and presence" - he seemed very ordinary. One witness testifies that a man once took him for a fool; Edmund's sharp response led the man, stunned by the repost, to say "I thought I had met a silly fellow but now I see that he is either a foolish scholar or a learned fool". He was authentically pious and prayerful, a determined believer who, according to another witness, had tremendous zeal for his faith and his mission. He was very witty, approaching difficulties and hardships, and even disputations, with a mischievous sense of humour. Physically he was a small man, and if we examine the only image we have of him - a portrait painted at some point in his priestly ministry - he looks robust and vigorous. At the time of his capture he mentioned he was weak and sick, and given that he almost died twice when in the seminary, we can conclude he may have been troubled with his health at times.

Return to Lancashire

Edmund's spirit, however, was strong, and when he returned to England he threw himself into his mission, and the field of that mission was Lancashire, in particular a wide geographical area around Brindle. Being a native, he could fit in quite comfortably; it was usual among these missionary priests to exercise their pastoral ministry in their native place. His accent would not betray him, nor his mannerisms or cultural habits; he knew the local dialects. As a son of the north living among his own, hiding in plain sight offered the best chance of safety and success. He knew the topography and where the Mass centres were. His family connections would be of great advantage to him, particularly his Gerard ancestry. He also knew where the hideouts were and how to get to them quickly. He adopted a number of aliases, Rigby and Bradshaw among them, to hide his real identity from strangers, of whom he had to be wary.

Unlike other parts of England, Lancashire was intensely Catholic and this was an advantage. While priests in other areas frequented the homes of the Catholic gentry, establishing their base within them and ministering to local Catholics who came to them, in Lancashire the missionary priest served among the ordinary people, going from house to house and farm to farm on horseback. Mass was celebrated in houses, barns and isolated places, usually at night so as not to attract attention. Local Catholics would be discreetly informed where the priest would be and when, and they would quietly make their way to the place. Sentinels would keep watch as the priest offered Mass and ministered to the flock. The people would then return home in the dead of night and the priest would leave the house at dawn and make his way to the next location for Mass that night. Such was the pattern of Edmund's life. He was constantly on the move. The road held many dangers for him, not just from priest-hunters and suspicious constables, but also from highwaymen who would see a suspected priest as easy prey.

Priest in disguise

We do not know what his cover was, but he was certainly in disguise. Priests on the English mission usually passed themselves off as officers home from military service, doctors or hired servants to gentlemen on their travels, or as sporting gentlemen - when Fr John Gerard first returned to England he pretended to be a gentleman looking for a lost falcon to get through an area of countryside without raising suspicions. When priests were based in homes of Catholic gentry they were disguised as tutors. Given his manner and stature Edmund's choice of disguise was limited, so he may have passed himself off as a doctor (a good cover to visit sick and dying Catholics) or as a travelling servant. Some missionary priests travelled with the company of a relative who acted as a servant, and this was the case for Edmund as one of his relations accompanied him throughout his ministry. Relatives proved more trustworthy than hired men, the bond of kinship guaranteeing greater fidelity and concern.

While we have few details of Edmund's ministry beyond the general pattern, various places in Lancashire are associated with him. Local traditions identify a number of places where he is believed to have offered Mass. He is said to have visited the village of Appleton near Widnes frequently for Mass; he is also said to have offered Mass in Salmesbury, Withnell, Wheelton, Clayton Green, Jack Green, Cuerdon and at Livesey Hall in Blackburn. He is believed to have baptised regularly at a holy well dedicated to St Helen in Whittle-le-woods near Preston. For fifteen years he was pastor, confessor and consoler of hundreds of Catholics, baptising, absolving, marrying and anointing the faithful. One of the ministries particularly associated with him was that of deliverance and exorcism. We are told that "Much pains he took with possessed persons, yet seldom or ever did he undergo that heavy and troublesome work without the help and assistance of some of his brethren, and so freed many from their troublesome yoke, and did much good."

Teaching the faith

Of his many duties, it is his preaching and defending the faith which most marks his ministry. He was renowned, including among Protestants, for his ability to teach the faith and to convert souls. Though his seminary studies were shortened for the sake of his health, he continued to study and he retained a great deal of knowledge. This, combined with a sharp intellect, a gift for speaking and his great zeal made him effective in disputation, which he never shied away from; indeed, he enjoyed it. Among the many traditions that have come down to us is one concerning a disputation Edmund was having with an Anglican minister. According to this story Edmund was conducting his defence of the faith with the Vicar of Brindle against the church wall. At one point Edmund declared: "If my religion is right, my foot will leave its impression on this stone", and setting his foot back against the wall he left the impression of his boot on the wall, no doubt with a grin on his face.

Edmund's friends feared for him at times. He was so capable, zealous and quick witted he could have easily got himself in trouble. One brother priest once advised him to be careful when disputing. He wrote:

Often I wished him merrily to carry salt in his pocket to season his actions, lest too much zeal without discretion might bring him too soon into danger, considering the vehement, sudden storms of persecution that often assailed us. Sometimes I have been in his company when meeting with ministers sumptuously mounted, and have had much ado to stay him from disputing with those proud dogs (so he was wont to call them), which if he had done it would have endangered, without doubt, both him and his company.

First arrest

For the many times he may have put himself in danger, it seems he was arrested only once before his call to martyrdom and that was during Lent of 1622. Arrested on suspicion of being a priest he was brought to Chester and for some reason it fell to the Anglican Bishop of Chester, then a Dr John Bridgeman, to interrogate him. When Edmund was brought before him Bridgeman was having supper with some of his vicars. As they were tucking into their meal the Bishop observed that Edmund had noticed that they were eating meat and he apologised to the priest saying that due to age and infirmity he was dispensed from

Jesuit

Accounts of Edmund's ministry tell us that for the first ten years of his ministry he lived his life as a good and conscientious secular priest, yet during that time he was reflecting on an important decision. He had not forgotten the retreat he made according to St Ignatius's Spiritual Exercises, and his interest in joining the ranks of the Society of Jesus had not waned. He was working with Jesuits on the mission and they impressed him by their way of life and holiness. He was already a holy man himself, but his heart yearned for something more; he wanted to make a deeper commitment to Christ by professing vows. Fr Cornelius Murphy writes: "He was resolved to make a full sacrifice of himself, he determined to reserve nothing of himself, not even his own will, offering himself up to God by religious vows, making self-denial, which the perfection of a religious state required, a preparation for his future martyrdom". By 1623 Edmund had made his decision to seek admission into the Society of Jesus.

At this point in time the Jesuits had been on the English mission for a short period; their presence was due to the efforts of William Allen to get this intrepid religious force into England to help turn the tide for Catholicism.

Portrait of Edmund Arrowsmith, St Mary's Wigan.

Having known Edmund Campion when he lived in the English College before he entered the Jesuits, Allen was convinced that a man of his calibre, and others like him, were necessary as an intellectual elite to combat heresy: after all, Allen mused, were they not founded to assist the Church respond to the Protestant revolution, and where better to do this than in England? During his visit to Rome in 1579-80 Allen was persuasive and he got his prize: Campion arrived back in England in 1581 with two brother Jesuits, Fr Robert Persons and Br Ralph Emerson, as an advance party. Though his ministry was short, Campion would open the door for his brother Jesuits. Mingling with the secular clergy and other regulars, these priests of the Society would prove effective and, in the eyes of the authorities, dangerous.

The Society of Jesus in England

By the 1620s the Society was well organised in England having divided the country into districts or 'colleges' each led by a rector. The first district established was that of London, which was dedicated to St Ignatius. Lancashire was part of the College of St Aloysius. Established in 1622, the college also included the counties of Cheshire, Westmorland and Stafford, and an average of twenty Jesuits were assigned to it at any one time. Fr John Worthington, William Allen's nephew, was appointed as its first rector, a post he would hold for twenty years.

Making contact with Fr Worthington, Edmund was examined and accepted for admission - his character and ministry, well known among the local clergy, stood him in good stead. He was sent to a house that served as a novitiate in Essex, where he was canonically received into the Society and began his formation. Given the situation in England he did not have the luxury of a long formation process. In the few months he spent there he made the month-long Spiritual Exercises, complemented a month later by studying the Constitutions of the Society among other things. When this brief period was over he made his Solemn Profession, professing with the vows of poverty, chastity and obedience, the fourth Jesuit vow of obedience to the Pope with regard to the mission and apostolic work of the Church. Before long he was back in the saddle in Lancashire.

In its external observance, Edmund's life did not change much for him as a Jesuit; he continued his pastoral work as per usual, visiting the communities he had been serving since he began his ministry. Interiorly there was a change: no longer a loner he was a member of a religious congregation, adhering to a particular charism and spirituality, a member of a community. In the Blue Anchor Inn at Brindle, their college's central house, he often gathered with his brother Jesuits, and there they supported each other in their religious life and ministry. Once a year he went on retreat for ten or twelve days to an isolated farm near Formby to rest, continue his formation as a son of St Ignatius and enjoy the company of his brothers. There was also another change: as bad as seminary priests were in the eyes of the authorities, Jesuits were worse. For Edmund the risks were increasing but his work was by no means diminishing. For the next five years he quietly worked and prayed, his life completely given into the hands of God.

Betrayal

It was issues of marriage and sex which led to Edmund's downfall; those who betrayed him were members of his own flock who were offended by his defence of Christian teaching in these areas. Given that the English reformation was founded on the very same issues, Edmund's experience is significant.

In the middle of August 1628 Edmund had arranged to offer Mass at a house on Gregson Lane, on the outskirts of Brindle; it has been suggested that it was either the 13th or 14th August. When Mass had finished, his plan was to retire to the Blue Anchor Inn perhaps for a rest and a meal. The Holden family owned the Blue Anchor Inn, which, as already noted, served as a centre and place of safety for Jesuits in the area. They were Catholics, and given the trust that the priests had put in them, they were faithful. The young son of the owner contracted a marriage with his cousin who was Protestant in a Protestant church. Perhaps it was through her contact with the priests who frequented the inn, but the young lady sought admission into the Church. She approached Edmund, who agreed to receive her, but he advised the pair that, given their close familial relationship, there was an impediment to their marriage.

Fortunately that could be dispensed from, but it would take time given that communication with Rome was not easy. It is worth noting that there may have been an unfortunate history here as the contemporary account indicates that Edmund had "often reproved the unhappy youth", young Holden, for being "obstinately entangled in sin".

Teaching on marriage

There are two versions of what happened next. The first relates how Edmund obtained the dispensation, but then asked the couple to separate for a fortnight before he would marry them - this may have been a condition laid down by Rome. The second version relates that he asked them to separate until the dispensation had been obtained. Either way the malice of the young man and, interestingly, his mother, was raised and they were determined to destroy the priest for his interference in the couple's relationship. One biographer has suggested that the young woman, now a Catholic, obeyed Edmund and denied the young man what he, regardless of the validity of their union, considered his conjugal rights. The young man and his mother wrote a letter to Captain Rawsthorn, the Justice of the Peace, informing him that a priest frequented the inn, and gave details as to when he would be there.

Though he was a Puritan and no friend of priests, Rawsthorn was concerned for Mr Holden, the innkeeper, whom he regarded as a friend. If a priest were found on his premises, and that priest had a custom of staying there, Holden might well be in danger himself, a fact that seems to have eluded his wife and son. Rawsthorn had no choice but to draw up a warrant, but he sent word ahead to say that he was coming to arrest the priest and the direction from which he would be coming. Mr Holden received the news with disgust, and soon as Edmund arrived from Gregson Lane he was warned of the danger and told to flee. Edmund and his servant grabbed their possessions and rode away at top speed. It has been suggested that he decided to make for Wickenhouse Farm, near Blackburn. He had often said Mass there and knew it to be isolated; he could hide there until it was safe to leave the area.

Flight and capture

The two left at top speed, but the flight was awkward; Edmund was laden down with clothes, books and a chest containing his vestments and Mass kit. He would have to hide the chest - if he was caught it would provide incontrovertible evidence that he was a priest. Meanwhile the pursuivants were catching up. Edmund and his servant turned into a large area of land known as Brindle Moss; there he spied a yew tree. He quickly dismounted, hid the chest in the trunk of the tree, remounted and headed towards a ditch which they had to clear to make their way towards the Blackburn road; from there a myriad of lanes would bring them to Wickenhouse Farm. The pursuivants, however, were gaining speed - they were now within sight. As he approached the ditch, Edmund's horse shied and refused to jump. After a couple of efforts, he dismounted, aiming to run with the horse to find a narrower crossing. Suddenly, to his horror, his servant rode off; the one he trusted most, a kinsman, had abandoned him. If the pursuivants caught up with him he would have to fight for himself and would most likely be captured. Fr Murphy suggests in his account that had the servant remained Edmund would have had a good chance of escape.

The first of the pursuivants arrived at the ditch, jumped off their horses, drew swords and struck out at him. Edmund, armed only with a walking stick, tried to parry the blows, but the stick was cut out of his hand and he was injured. He tried to run, but they were too quick for him; he was caught, overpowered and pinned down. The remaining pursuivants arrived and he was tied up. They made their way to a local inn, the Boar's Head, and there they searched him "to the skin", as he said himself, making some sort of sexual advances which he tried to stave off. He was carrying nine shillings in his purse which they confiscated to fuel a night's drinking. He was then locked up in an outhouse, where he spent the night still trussed up. The next morning, he was conveyed to Lancaster Castle.

Unconfined zeal

On arrival Edmund was committed to the care of the keeper of the castle, Thomas Covell, who was a magistrate but also mayor of Lancaster that year. Since it was suspected that he was a priest, the oaths of Supremacy and Allegiance were presented to him, but he refused to take them. Admitted into the general population of the prison to await trial, Edmund discovered that his friends Dom Ambrose Barlow and Fr John Southworth were also imprisoned. Though incarcerated, providentially as Edmund would see it, this period gave the friends time to converse and encourage each other. Edmund's pastoral zeal was not dampened either, as Fr Murphy relates:

> Although the holy missionary's body was confined, his zeal could not be. He gave himself no rest in gaol. His charity and zeal for souls continued; he exhorted the prisoners to their duty and his words had such power that felons became his friends. He preached the Gospel to them with success, and converted one, who followed him in his death, and had a share in his glory.

The man he converted was a horse-thief.

Among the others he ministered to was the farmer Richard Hurst who was indicted on a false charge of murder. Long known for his adherence to Catholicism, Richard was regularly visited by pursuivants. During one of these visits there was a fracas between some of his employees and the pursuivants leading to one of the pursuivants falling from his horse and breaking his leg. The wound proved fatal, though before he died the doomed man stressed that the fall was simply an unfortunate accident. The death, however, was deemed fortunate by the authorities, a convenient excuse to have Richard put on trial for his faith. He was arrested and charged with murder. He would be tried, condemned to death and martyred the day after Edmund.

Trial

Sir Henry Yelverton was the judge scheduled to preside over the Assizes in Lancaster that summer of 1628; it fell to him to try both Edmund and Richard Hurst. Yelverton was one of those interesting men whose lives are lived in the background of history and who yet, in their time, were noteworthy, touching as they did events and figures central to any age. Edmund and Yelverton had an interesting connection. Fr John Gerard, Edmund's cousin, had reconciled the judge's aunt, Jane Lumner, to the Catholic faith; she had been Calvinist. Yelverton came from a religiously divided family; one side was Catholic, the other extreme Calvinist; he was a Puritan himself. To understand this judge's view of Edmund and Catholicism, it is necessary to understand his life and experiences.

The eldest son of the judge Sir Christopher Yelverton, one of the leaders of the Calvinists in England, Henry is recorded as having been educated by graduates of Oxford University before being admitted to Gray's Inn in 1579. It has been surmised that Henry and his brother Christopher may have been admitted by favour rather than merit. He was elected Member of Parliament for the borough of Northampton in 1604, King James I's first parliament, but that career was not entirely successful due to his erratic nature and frequent change of opinion on various issues - this instability of judgement was not conducive to a political career. His rough common sense led him to adopt the popular objections to the royal proceedings in detail, so he was frequently in trouble. Early on he publicly opposed the king in championing one MP the king was attempting to have rejected from his seat; he lost that battle and James's favour, as he did again in the 1606-1607 session of parliament, when he found himself defying the king once more as he attacked one of the king's favourites, the Earl of Dunbar.

The man to condemn a priest to death

Thanks to Sir Francis Bacon, then Solicitor General, Yelverton's star began to rise. Over the next few years he rose as Bacon rose, stepping into the offices Bacon had just vacated: Solicitor General in 1613 and Attorney General in 1617. In that latter year Bacon had become Lord Chancellor of England and Yelverton may well have had his eye on that office. It would be his insecurity which led to his downfall. In a matter concerning a revolt by merchants against the Crown's monopoly of gold and silver thread, Yelverton, with a cautious eye to his advancement, was hesitant to bear responsibility for the merchants' incarceration - an unpopular development in the eyes of the populace. In an effort to ensure someone would cover his back, he announced that he would release the merchants unless the Lord Chancellor, Bacon, would stand by him and support him. Bacon was furious. Recently discovering that Yelverton had passed a charter for the City of London containing unauthorised provisions, Bacon used this as an excuse to initiate legal proceedings against him. In his defence Yelverton implicated the King's favourite, the Duke of Buckingham, and so began his fall from grace; he was committed to the Tower of London, earned the king's fury and was dismissed from office. Brought to trial before the House of Lords on 16th May 1621 he was sentenced to imprisonment and fined. He was released the following July, a man with no prospects. But all was not lost; following James's death and the accession of Charles I in 1625, he was appointed a judge - a fifth judge of the Court of Common Pleas. It was this position which brought him to the Lancaster Assizes in August of 1628.

It was a rancorous man, one not inclined to mercy, who arrived into Lancaster on the 25th August to preside over a suspected priest's trial. To confound matters, just before he left London for the Assizes, some of his friends, when they discovered he was about to try an alleged priest, joked that he would not dare, giving the tolerant climate that prevailed, condemn a priest to death. Stung by these remarks he was intent on proving them wrong. A first reading of Fr Murphy's contemporary account of Edmund's trial might lead us to conclude that its depiction of Henry Yelverton is more caricature than reality, however, given the vicissitudes he faced and his, by now, caustic view of life and his failures, not to mention his Puritanism and his view of Catholicism, it was not only an unhappy man on the bench, but an angry and bitter one.

Edmund's trial

On Tuesday 26th August, early in the morning, as Edmund was conversing with friends, the gaoler arrived to inform him that he was summoned to court that day. Edmund cheerfully responded, "God's holy will be done". Calm and restrained, though he was suffering from severe toothache, he was taken under armed guard to the courtroom. When Yelverton came into the court he took one look at Edmund and immediately sent word for a brother judge, Sir James Whitelocke,[4] to join him on the bench. Whitelocke shared many of Yelverton's views, including his opinion on abolishing the royal prerogative.

With the jury in place, Yelverton immediately got down to business: "Sir, are you a priest?" Edmund made the sign of the cross; "I would to God I were worthy", he replied. This was the stock answer priests were instructed to use when on trial; it was one that evaded the issue: not a lie, but not yielding the truth either. Yelverton asked again, Edmund replied, "I would I were". The judge drew conclusions: "Yes, he is not, but desires to be a traitor!" He then framed the question in the negative and asked if he was not a priest. Edmund did not answer, leading Yelverton to address the jury: "You may easily see he is a priest. I warrant you he would not for all England deny his order". Edmund could not affirm that he was a priest, to do so did not merely endanger his own life, but in affirming his status he would have placed all those who knew him and sheltered him in danger.

"You shall die!"

At this point a parson and a Justice of the Peace, Mr Leigh, approached the bench. He knew Edmund or "Mr Rigby", as it was thought he was, and he had information for the judge: he remembered him from the encounter with the Bishop of Chester six years before. He attacked the priest and claimed he was a seducer who would convert half of Lancashire if he got the chance, a compliment for Edmund if ever there was one. Edmund asked if he could defend his faith by means of a disputation with Leigh, but the request was denied, to which Edmund responded that he would not only defend his faith with words, but would be glad to seal it with his blood. "You shall seal it with your blood", Yelverton replied, saying he would ensure that the prisoner would be executed and see his bowels burnt before his face. "You shall die!" Yelverton shouted. "And you, my Lord, must die", Edmund quietly replied.

Yelverton then asked him to justify his going beyond the seas, in disobedience to the law, to be ordained a priest. Edmund responded: "If any man can lawfully accuse me, I stand ready here to answer him". At this point the evidence was produced. First there was the letter from Mrs Holden and her son to Captain Rawsthorn. Though this was confirmation that there was a Jesuit priest at the Blue Anchor, it did not identify Edmund specifically; more evidence was required. Two witnesses were called, the first a servant of the Justice who was involved in the committal of the prisoner. This witness testified that Edmund had tried to persuade him to become a Catholic telling him "that the religion now professed in England was heretical and only began in Luther's time". However, he could not offer evidence to say Edmund was a priest. The second witness was Rawsthorn's son who was twelve years old; given his age he was excused the oath. He testified that the prisoner would have drawn him from the Protestant religion; again, apart from this accusation the child had no evidence to prove Mr Rigby was a Jesuit priest.

Edmund's speech

Edmund asked if he could defend himself, leave was given and he then relayed what had happened when he was arrested:

> My Lord, as I was upon the road that very man, as I take it, rushed out upon me by a hillside with a drawn sword.

He was meanly dressed and on horseback. I made what haste I could from him, but being weak and sickly, he forced me at last to the moss where I dismounted and fled with all the speed I was able, though that was not very great, seeing as I was loaded with heavy clothes, books and other things. At length he came up to me at a moss ditch, he struck at me, though I had nothing to defend me but a little walking stick and a sword which I did not draw. With a blow he cut the stick close to my hand and did me some little hurt. I then asked him whether his design was to take my purse and my life. He answered that perhaps it was; upon which I fled again from him but was soon overtaken. Then came this youth, who has offered to give evidence against me, and others to assist him. They used me very unworthily and carried me first to an alehouse and searched me to the skin offering indignities which modesty forbids me to relate and I resisted as I was able. That done, they fell to drinking, spent nine shillings of my money in one hour, and told me that the Justice by whose warrant I was apprehended was there in person; but that I knew not how to believe. Upon this occasion, my Lords, I began to find fault with this man's wicked and rude behaviour, who seemed to be the ringleader, and I besought him for Jesus' sake to give over his disordered life, drinking, dissolute talk and whatever might offend Almighty God. Upon my word and upon my life, this or to this effect is all I said to him. Let him look at me and gainsay if he can. As for that youth, I deny not to have told him that I hoped, when he came to riper years, he would look better into himself and become a true Catholic for that, and that alone, would be the means to save his soul. To this he made no answer at all. And I hope, my Lords, that neither they nor any can prove any ill thing against me.

Conclusion of the trial and verdict

This speech elicited a fierce invective from the Justice who accused Edmund of being "a dangerous seducer" and he was sure that if the prisoner was ever freed he would do him [the Justice] "some mischief". Edmund smiled at the thought of it, leading Yelverton to accuse him of being a "saucy fellow", laughing at and flouting those who sat in judgment for the king. Edmund asked the court not to harbour that opinion and going on his knees he prayed for the king, the honourable bench, and all people that heresy would be confounded and they all would be united in the one faith. Yelverton using this to his advantage addressed the jury: "Look you, Gentlemen of the jury, how he wishes God to confound us all and to root out heresy by which he means our religion".

Yelverton had had enough. He had made his position clear to the jury, now they had to deliver the verdict - the deliberation would be merely a matter of course. As it was dinner time the jury was given leave to withdraw, Yelverton and Whitelocke went to their chambers for their meal and Edmund was sent back to his cell. He was glad of the break; the toothache was getting worse and he needed a rest. Food was brought to him, but the pain was so bad he found it difficult to eat much of it; by the time he was called back to court the meal had hardly been touched.

When the jury returned, they delivered a verdict of guilty of high treason. Satisfied, Yelverton, as required by custom, asked the condemned what he had to say for himself and why he should not be put to death in accordance with the law; Edmund remained silent. Whitelocke retired, leaving it to Yelverton to pass sentence: for his priesthood he was to be hanged, drawn and quartered, his remains hung upon the castle walls as a warning to others tempted to disregard the laws of the kingdom.

Deo gratias

Edmund fell to his knees, bowed his head and gave thanks to God: "Deo gratias. God be thanked." Yelverton was not finished: he ordered that the priest be shackled in the heaviest irons they could find and put into a dungeon without light and far from human company. Informed there was no such place in the castle, he directed that he be put in the worst cell they had. As he was being taken out Edmund prayed the *Miserere*, Psalm 50. He was led to a tiny cell, too small even for him; he could not lie down nor find any comfort in it. It seems he received no food from that day until his death. He was watched day and night by the guards, who had been warned not to show him any kindness: Yelverton ordered that no one was permitted access to him under pain of substantial fines.

Earlier in his imprisonment Edmund had written a letter in which he explained how he understood the work of God in his life. Discerning what was happening, he wrote with complete surrender: "All particulars did so cooperate in my apprehension and bringing me herewith that I can discern more than an ordinary providence therein." In that little cell, in silence, discomfort and pain, he prepared himself for the fulfilment of that providence.

Witness

Thursday 28th August 1628 was an overcast and dreary day reflecting, as it turned out, the gloom that had descended on Lancaster. As soon as the people had heard of the sentence imposed on "Mr Rigby" a sense of shock had quickly evolved into horror and disgust, and as the two days following the trial passed these feelings manifested themselves in a refusal by the entire population to have anything to do with what was about to happen. There were some denizens who believed Edmund would be brought to the gallows and reprieved; after all it was well known that King Charles abhorred the shedding of blood on religious grounds.

Those organising the execution realised they had a problem: no one in the town was prepared to lend them an axe to carry out the deed - a sure sign not only of people's abhorrence, but also of a clemency that had existed long enough for the authorities not to include such an instrument in their arsenal. Finding an executioner was even more difficult, but eventually a butcher agreed to carry out the deed. On reflection and fearing a backlash for his participation, the butcher leaned on one of his employees to take his place; the young man fled the town never to be seen again: he would not have innocent blood on his hands.

Edmund in prison

The same climate prevailed in the prison. During his short time among them Edmund had impressed his fellow inmates. His innocence of life, kindness and wit, not to mention his genuine piety, had endeared him to usually hardened criminals. Locked away in his cramped cell, Edmund's fellow prisoners were horrified at the conditions he was enduring, alone and starving. When the authorities, having failed to employ an executioner in the town, turned to the prisoners, no promises or reprieves would convince them to take the job. One finally relented, a soldier who had deserted the army and was under sentence of death. Promised a pardon, his freedom and Edmund's clothes he agreed to act as executioner. The problem of an axe remained, one was eventually found somewhere outside Lancaster. During those two days Mr Leigh arrived at the door of Edmund's cell to dispute with him, but he was turned away - Edmund suspected that Leigh, knowing he could not be moved, might well use the opportunity to spread the lie that he had conformed.

Henry Yelverton was having problems of his own. Having passed the sentence of death he had to have a warrant drawn up before the execution could be carried out. The sheriff, however, had issues with the unorthodox

P. Edmundus Arousmithæus Angl, Soc: IESV pro Fide Ca=
tholica suspensus, et dissectus Lancastriæ in Anglia. 7. Sept. A. 1628.

The execution of Edmund Arrowsmith.

manner in which the trial had been carried out: it was obvious the whole affair had been unjust, so he refused to issue a warrant. Unperturbed Yelverton wrote up the commission himself and sent it to his colleague, Sir James Whitelocke, to read and sign. Whitelocke refused to sign it sending the document back with the request that Yelverton sign it first. Furious, Yelverton, true to form, drew up what was an illegal warrant, one in which he and the other participants might be absolved of the part they were playing in the condemnation. In this warrant he removed explicit reference to himself and Whitelocke, merely referring to "the Court sitting" and "ordered by the Court" with regard to sentence - no names, no qualms of conscience, no burden of guilt, just anonymous justice.

Witnesses to the execution

At around 8 am Edmund was informed by the sheriff that he was to die within four hours. Yelverton's original intention was to execute him very early in the morning to avoid a gathering; he feared a reaction from the populace. Preparations did not go as planned, so he rescheduled the execution for noon when most people would be at home having dinner. This did not work out either: all the businesses in the town shut down and crowds began to form along the route the procession of the condemned would take to Gallows Hill. Many would be present to protest at what was happening; some to see that the sentence was carried out and England was cleared of another "seditious Jesuit"; others for curiosity's sake. Then there were Catholics, perhaps some to whom Edmund had ministered; they were present as witnesses to the martyrdom, to pray for him, be edified and to preserve his memory. Among them was an anonymous eyewitness who would later record all that happened.

In his cell Edmund was calm and recollected; the news brought by the sheriff did not disturb him. With perfect resignation he simply responded, with fervour, "I beseech my Redeemer to make me worthy of it". He made his preparations, writing out on two pieces of paper an act of love of God and an act of contrition, the "two keys of heaven"; when the time came he could pray these from the notes rather than rely on his memory should stress overwhelm him. He had no property to will to anyone; indeed, even if he had, his conviction for treason would have meant all his possessions were forfeit to the Crown. His very body would be the property of the authorities and they would hack it to pieces; all he had for himself was his soul and in these last hours he was preparing to offer that, for the last time, to God.

Absolution

At about 11 a.m. the gaoler arrived to conduct him to the sheriff. As he was being led out he passed a young woman, Margery, a maid whose Catholic parents lived in part of the prison. She stood still with respect as he was being tied to the hurdle. Asking her if she wanted anything of him, she replied she wanted nothing but his company. He encouraged her to continue to practise her faith and without question she would be counted among the Blessed in heaven. As he was being led through the yard Fr John Southworth was standing at an open window. Edmund had arranged with him to grant him final absolution just before the execution. Edmund lifted up his hands, the sign they had agreed upon, and Fr John prayed the formula of absolution over him. Fr John would be released a short time later and would minister for a number of years before suffering martyrdom at Tyburn in 1654.

Once he was tied to the hurdle the sombre procession began, Edmund being dragged through the streets behind a horse. Usually the condemned would be situated feet facing the horse, head at the end near the ground; in Edmund's case, as an act of degradation Yelverton ordered he be positioned in the opposite direction, his head right at the horse's backside for ignominy's sake. In his hands Edmund held the "two keys to heaven". He was well guarded, the executioner walking ahead, the sheriff and heavily armed guards surrounding him. Despite this an elderly Catholic gentleman broke through to embrace and kiss him tenderly until he was dragged away by guards.

As they passed through the streets there were none of the usual insults. The atmosphere was pensive. As they passed an inn, The Golden Lion, not far from Gallows Hill, a mug of beer was brought to him. Since its foundation in 1612 the innkeeper observed a custom of offering a last drink to the condemned as an act of charity. This time the condemned refused it; perhaps Edmund had in mind the words of Jesus: "I will not drink from henceforth of this fruit of the vine, until that day when I shall drink it with you new in the kingdom of my Father".[5]

Gallows Hill

When they arrived at Gallows Hill, everything was ready for the execution. Many still expected a decree of reprieve would be read and the condemned man returned to prison. Even if King Charles had heard about Edmund, Yelverton was intent on having the sentence carried out. No reprieve would be forthcoming anyway: Charles was in difficulty, he was appealing to parliament to help resolve his financial problems and parliament, mostly Puritans, was using the king's weakness to ensure that the penal laws against Catholics, for so long ignored, were enforced. Edmund's indictment had come at the wrong time; Charles could not show mercy even if he wanted to. The king would lose his own head to these same parliamentarians in the not too distant future.

A cauldron was boiling beside the gallows - his head and quartered body would be partially cooked in it to preserve them for display over the coming months. The parson-

Justice of the Peace Leigh was keen to bring the cauldron to Edmund's attention, pleading, "Will you conform and lay hold of the King's mercy?" Edmund smiled, "Good sir, tempt me no more. The mercy which I look for is in heaven through the death and passion of my Saviour, Jesus Christ; and I humbly beg Him to make me worthy of this death".

Edmund's prayer

He was dragged to the foot of the ladder which leaned against the gallows; he would be made to ascend the rungs and then, noose around his neck, be pushed off. First, he was given time "to make his peace with God". Edmund knelt on the ground for fifteen minutes and prayed silently. Standing up, and then kneeling three times he prayed: "I freely and willingly offer to thee, sweetest Jesus, this my death in satisfaction for my sins, and I wish that this little blood of mine may be a sacrifice for them". Some clergymen who stood around him objected strongly to what he was praying and tried to interrupt him several times, but Edmund was oblivious to them. When he had finished the prayer they charged him with blasphemy, but Edmund refuted their claims, and continued praying.

The contemporary document records the prayer which followed; it has become known as his "Offering of Self":

O Jesus, my life and my glory, I cheerfully restore the life which I have received from Thee, and, was it not thy gift, would not be mine to return. I have ever desired, O

God of my Soul, to resign my life to Thee, and for Thee.
The loss of life for Thy sake, I own my advantage, and
the preservation of it without Thee, my ruin. I die for
love of Thee; for our holy faith; for the support of the
authority of Thy Vicar on earth, the successor of St
Peter, true head of the Catholic Church, which Thou
hast founded and established. My sins, O Lord, were
the cause of Thy death. In my death I only desire Thee,
who art true life. Permit not, most merciful Jesus, that
I escape torments to live without Thee. Life can be no
advantage, where Thou art not. Give me, Good Jesus,
constancy to the last moment, let me not live one instant
without Thee; for since Thou art true life, I cannot live,
unless Thou livest in me. When I reflect that I have
offended Thee, I am seized with greater grief than can
be caused by the loss of my life. O life of my whole life!
but how of my whole life, if I have ever offended Thee?
However, with true sorrow I wholly devote myself to
Thee, and with all my heart forgive those who take my
life away, and by that means, give me this opportunity
to resign it into Thy sacred hands.

"God's holy will be done"

After offering this prayer, not without attempts to interrupt
him, which he ignored, he kissed the ladder, "God's holy
will be done", he said, and began to ascend the rungs. He
asked Catholics present to join their prayers with him and

support him, but Leigh interjected with the claim that there were no Catholics present but that he would pray for him. Edmund replied, decisively, "I neither desire your prayers nor will I pray with you. I will have nothing to do with you, and if what you say be true, that there are no Catholics here, I wish to die as many deaths as there are people here on condition that they were all Catholics". He prayed for the king, the kingdom and his persecutors, once again forgiving them, and asked forgiveness of those he himself had offended.

Advancing a little more up the ladder, Edmund declared:

Bear witness, gentlemen, who are come to see my end, that I die a constant Roman Catholic and for Jesus Christ his sake, let not my death be a hindrance to your well doing, and going forward in the Catholic religion, but rather encourage you thereto. For Jesus' sake, have a care of your souls, than which nothing is more precious; and become members of the true Church, as you tender your salvation; for thereafter, that alone will do you good. I beseech you, request my brethren, for His sake, who redeemed us all, to be careful to supply my want and insufficiency, as I hope they will. Nothing grieves me so much, as this England, which I pray God soon to convert.

He turned to pray the "two keys of heaven" from the papers in his hands, and then pulled a little cap he was wearing over his eyes to resume his silent prayer.

"Good Jesus"

Leigh was in no mood to be conquered by this piety and tried to disturb Edmund again, urging him to recant and "accept the King's mercy"; if only he took the Oath of Allegiance his life would be spared. "I desire you to live", Leigh pleaded. "Here is a man come from the Judge to offer you mercy. You may live if you will conform to the Protestant religion". Edmund, drawing his cap from his eyes, dismissed him: "O sir, how far am I from that! Tempt me no more. I am a dying man. I will do it in no case, on no condition". Turning to the sheriff he said, "The day will come when far from repenting your return to the Catholic Church, you will find it your greatest comfort and advantage".

Some in the crowd by now had had enough and urged the executioner to do his job: "No more of that!" they shouted, "No more of that! Away with him!" Edmund composed himself and was lost in prayer when he was pushed from the ladder. The last words from his lips were "Bone Jesu. Good Jesus." The contemporary account relates that he "suffered to hang until his soul was admitted to the crown of justice which is laid up for God's faithful servants". This would seem to imply that Edmund was already dead before he was cut down and the mutilation began. To ensure no relics could be gathered his blood was swept up with sand and burnt. Despite precautions taken, no one noticed the cautious, unknown witness who laid hold of the martyr's right hand and secreted it away.

Following the execution

Yelverton did not attend the execution. Safely guarded in Covell's house, a fine dinner waiting for him, he watched the proceedings from the window through a spyglass, sitting down to his meal when the mutilation was finished. As he was eating, some men arrived with a gift of venison for him, and a few moments later the executioners came with Edmund's remains. For some unknown reason he handled both venison and remains together, comparing the two. He ordered that the head be set on a pinnacle of the castle (he would later demand it be raised higher) and the quarters displayed on the walls to remain until they perished. He then finished his dinner. The next day he left for London, his work done. He died over a year later, on 29th January 1630, in mysterious circumstances.

The people of Lancaster returned to their homes. Many were appalled by what they had seen. Fr Murphy notes: "Many Protestants, moved by his fortitude and patience, wished their souls with him who then died. Others either out of remorse or detestation of this bloody act repented their coming to the spectacle. Some judged it very laudable to be constant to their religion, but thought it too great a stretch of obligation to die for that cause. Some touched with compassion esteemed it barbarous to use a person thus for his religion". Catholics in the crowd were edified and encouraged in their faith, and the cult of the martyr, Fr Edmund Arrowsmith, began. There was one disgruntled man in the midst of it all. Despite the promises made to him, the executioner was returned to prison; his freedom would be granted, eventually. In the meantime he had to comfort himself in his cell with the few clothes the man he had killed had worn.

Glory

As young Margery, the maid whom Edmund had comforted, was asleep in her room the night after the execution, her roommate was woken by sighs. "Lord, Mr Rigby," Margery said in her sleep, "in what a stately place is this where you now live, which is so bright, composed of silver and gold; would God I might remain with you, for methinks the place is most sweet, like flowers of perfumes". When she woke next morning, her friend, remembering what she had said, questioned her, but Margery could not remember anything.

That same night, Dom Ambrose Barlow was staying at Morleys Hall, near Astley, Greater Manchester having just been released unexpectedly from Lancaster Castle. He was as yet unaware that his friend had been executed. As he related by letter to his brother, Dom Rudesind, many years later, he was sleeping and was suddenly awoken, and to his surprise Edmund was standing by his bedside. "I have suffered", Edmund told him, "and now you will be to suffer; say little, for they will endeavour to take hold of your words". Ambrose would cherish the memory of this apparition for the rest of his life. The prophetic words were fulfilled on 10th September 1641 when he was martyred in the same way as Edmund, also in Lancaster on Gallows Hill.

Relics of a martyr

Other miraculous events occurred following the execution. The father of Fr John Southworth, who was present at the execution, reported seeing, at the moment of Edmund's death, a light streaming from the place of execution along the road the martyr had travelled right back to the castle, the gloomy nature of the weather highlighting the brightness of this light. At the house on Gregson Lane a cross of light appeared in the room where Edmund had offered his last Mass; this phenomenon continues intermittently to this day. Greater miracles were yet to come, and foremost among them were the conversions which occurred as his life and witness became known.

As Edmund's remains perished on the walls of Lancaster Castle, the unknown devotee brought the hand to his mother. She preserved it, wrapped in linen, until her death when she bequeathed it to her family; it remained in the possession of the Gerards until entrusted in the 19th century to the parish church of St Oswald in Ashton-in-Makerfield, where it remains. The linen in which the hand was preserved was changed every so often, and as devotees requested pieces of the old material as relics a tradition of blessing linen with the hand developed. These relics would become instrumental in various miracles and favours granted through Edmund's intercession. This Blessed Linen is still distributed from the shrine in Ashton.

Growing devotion

Biographers note that other relics were also obtained. One gentleman, Henry Holme, testifies in a letter to a Thomas Metcalfe in 1629 that he had persuaded plumbers working at Lancaster Castle to take some hair and pieces of ribs from the remains as they were engaged in mending lead plumbing. He also records that as the quarters were being taken from the gallows, someone managed to have a handkerchief dipped in Edmund's blood. Other blood relics were obtained thanks to Protestants who dipped pieces of straw in blood and gave them to their Catholic friends. With regards to Edmund's possessions, few remain. The vestments and Mass kit which he had hidden in the yew tree at Brindle Moss were discovered in 1832 when a violent storm blew it down; they are now on display at Stonyhurst College. His statue of Our Lady, which had fallen from him as he was chased at the Moss, was recovered some time after his capture and is still preserved. A number of altars around Lancashire are associated with him and other missionary priests.

Edmund's holiness and martyrdom remained fixed in the hearts of Catholics in Lancashire and in England, and would spread beyond to Ireland and the Continent. He was honoured at the English College, Douai, as one of its most illustrious alumni and martyrs - the news of his martyrdom arrived at the college a few months later on 6th November.

The Jesuits revered his memory and propagated his heroic witness in their missionary work. Devotion grew and miracles were worked leading persecuted Catholics to venerate him as a saint. Miracles continue to occur and are reported regularly; indeed, given the numerous favours granted through his intercession, he might be aptly called *Thaumaturgus*, 'wonder-worker'.

Canonisation

The Church, however, would take some time to officially recognise him as such. Work on a cause for the martyrs of the English Reformation, from the time of Henry VIII up to the 17th century began tentatively around 1643. Edmund's martyrdom was examined with that of 233 others in a cause that was introduced in 1923 and came to a conclusion on 15th December 1929 when he and 135 of these companions were beatified by Pope Pius XI. On 1st December 1960 a petition was submitted to the Holy See to give permission for a group of forty martyrs to be advanced as a single cause: Blessed Edmund among them. In August 1962 a young mother from Mill Hill, Blackburn in Lancashire claimed to have been miraculously healed of a malignant tumour, a fibrosarcoma of the left scapula, after praying to the Forty Martyrs. Following a formal process of investigation this healing was found to be 'gradual, perfect, constant and without medical explanation'. Blessed Pope Paul VI approved the authenticity of the healing.

On Sunday 25th October 1970, Edmund was canonised a Saint in St Peter's Square, one of the Forty Martyrs of England and Wales. Among those raised to the altars with him on that day were his hero and namesake, Edmund Campion, and his friends and fellow missionaries, Ambrose Barlow and John Southworth.

Endnotes

[1] Letter of William Chaderton, Anglican Bishop of Chester, to the Privy Council in 1583.

[2] Sir Thomas Gerard was known to have been a Catholic; he was the father of the Jesuit, Fr John Gerard. A supporter of Mary, Queen of Scots, Sir Thomas was implicated in one of the plots to rescue her; for his troubles he was imprisoned in the Tower of London. Released, and having lost some of his property, Sir Thomas moved to Bryn near Haydock, with his children. He was imprisoned again for his alleged part in the Babington Plot to assassinate Elizabeth and put Mary, Queen of Scots, on the English throne. Following his release from prison in 1588 he abandoned his faith; conforming to the state church; however, he would return to Catholicism before his death.

[3] Some accounts of St Edmund's life record his baptismal name as Barnaby; the contemporary document of 1630 favours Brian.

[4] In the contemporary account his name is rendered as Whitlock.

[5] Matt 26:29, Douai-Reims version.